De Gaulle ⚜ ⚜

Brian Crozier

De Gaulle

Charles Scribner's Sons · New York

Contents

Author's Note and Acknowledgements   ix

PART I: THE ENIGMA OF DE GAULLE

1   The Man   3
2   Historical Prologue   10

PART II: HISTORIAN AND THINKER 1890–1939

1   Pupil of the Jesuits (1890–1909)   17
2   The Young Officer (1909–1918)   23
3   The Historian (1919–1924)   32
4   Pétain's Protégé (1924–1932)   41
5   A Prophet Ignored (1932–1939)   57

PART II: FREE FRANCE 1939–1945

1   The Defeat (1939–1940)   83
2   The Challenge   109
3   The Free French   119
4   Divided They Fall   134
5   De Gaulle versus his Allies: 1   144
6   De Gaulle versus his Allies: 2   165
7   Roosevelt in the Ascendant   183
8   "Torch" and After   195
9   Casablanca   207
10   Algiers   222
11   The Resistance   235
12   Roots of the Fourth Republic   246
13   The Agony of France   259

PART IV: THE LIBERATION AND AFTER 1944–1946

1 Jostling for Position 273
2 De Gaulle's Parisian Triumph 295
3 Trial of Strength 317
4 Foreign Disappointments 329
5 International Discords 349
6 Vichy on Trial 368
7 The Patient Stirs 375
8 De Gaulle Steps Down 385

PART V: THE FOURTH REPUBLIC 1946–1958

1 Birth and Challenge 399
2 Triumph and Collapse 419
3 In the Wilderness 441
4 De Gaulle Returns 453

PART VI: THE FIFTH REPUBLIC

1 De Gaulle breaks the Opposition (1958–1962) 481
2 The Atlantic Directorate Affair 520
3 Europe and the World 545
4 The Pressure Mounts 569
5 The Roots of Discontent 590
6 Storm and Aftermath 616
7 Exit and Death 646

PART VII: DE GAULLE IN HISTORY

1 Man and Showman 663
2 Soldier and Writer 666
3 Politician and Statesman 672

Bibliographical Note 687

Index 705

Author's Note
and Acknowledgements

To claim a love-hate relationship with the French is not unusual, but the phrase does apply to me. I spent seven years of my childhood in France, six of them at school in the Lycée at Montpellier. At twelve, I spoke English badly and with a strong French accent. Now I am bilingual enough to be taken for French in France and to use occasional Gallicisms in English. Some of my best friends are French, and so are some of the people I have most cordially detested. This alone gives me something in common with the subject of this book.

My attitude towards General de Gaulle is, perhaps, similarly ambivalent. In common with most people of the British Isles who lived through the Second World War, I was emotionally stirred by de Gaulle's decision to fight on after France's stunning defeat. I remained, broadly speaking, a "Gaullist" throughout the war, and was intolerant of Roosevelt's doubts, and of his obtuseness in preferring Giraud: I never doubted that de Gaulle would come out on top in Algiers, and of course he did.

My admiration for de Gaulle did not, however, extend to his followers, whom I found irritatingly self-righteous. In recent years, and with honourable exceptions, I have found self-righteousness to be a continuing characteristic of the Gaullist movement. To claim superiority over that vast majority of the French people who initially sided with Marshal Pétain was, of course, a pardonable conceit in men who took pride in upholding France's honour; but I have always been less tolerant of the assumption that Gaullists are superior to non-Frenchmen as well.

As for General de Gaulle himself, my experience in writing his biography has been the opposite of that of writing Franco's life. With Franco, I started from a point of hostility, discovered how profoundly he had been misrepresented and reached the stage of "grudging admiration". With de Gaulle, while my admiration for the man of June 1940 remains, to compile the inventory of his later aberrations is to be deeply disillusioned.

The personality, the will and the skill, the erudition and the self-discipline, the memory and the courage: these things still kindle the admiration. But the harm he did the West, and therefore France, outlives him. I hope this book makes it clear that it is possible to admire the man and to deplore much of what he did or failed to do. To those of my French friends who are also Gaullists, I tender my apologies. I hope only that they will recognise the care I have taken to be objective.

Although no other study of de Gaulle's entire life had appeared when this book was completed, his career is richly documented. Some entirely new material did, however, come my way, both in the form of documents and in that of personal reminiscences, orally expressed.

Many of the well-placed people who told me what they knew, especially about Franco-German, Franco-British and Franco-American relations during de Gaulle's second period of power, asked to remain anonymous. I have respected their wishes, and simply attributed the relevant matter to "private source" or "private information". I wish to emphasise that these anonymous informants are of several nationalities.

Among those who did not ask me to conceal their names are the following, to whom I express my thanks: MM. Jacques Baumel, Roger Frey, Louis Joxe, Pierre Mendès France, Gaston Palewski, Jean Sainteny, Jacques Soustelle and Louis Vallon. I am grateful to Major-General Sir Edward Spears for his kind permission to quote from a wartime report of his on de Gaulle and the Free French. And I owe a special debt of gratitude to Mrs A. D. Lacy, who kindly gave me access to the papers of her late husband, Commander A. D. Lacy, relating to his service as naval liaison officer to the then commander of the Free French naval forces, Admiral Muselier. This important collection, of which I have made a selective use, throws a new light on the successive "Muselier affairs".

Thanks are also due to my research assistant, Judith Miller, without whose help I would not have been able to complete the copy on time; and to Mrs Dorothy Pickles, who took on the daunting task of reading the entire typescript and commenting on it in detail. I owe much to her knowledge and advice; any remaining errors or oddities of judgment are, of course, entirely my own responsibility. As always, the staff of the London Library and of Chatham House were admirably cooperative. The Quai d'Orsay was courteous but unwilling to depart from its fifty-year rule of official secrecy. The French official historian, M. Henri Michel, was courteously helpful and kindly gave me access to his material on Free France and the Resistance. My thanks are due to him, as they are to the staffs of the Association Nationale pour le Soutien à l'Action du Général de Gaulle, and of the Photothèque of the French Armed Forces at Ivry.

I did not meet General de Gaulle. I had been promised an audience in May 1969, on the assumption that he would have won the referendum of April and would still be in power. He lost, and was not. In our subsequent exchanges of letters, he agreed to answer any questions I might send him at Colombey-les-Deux-Eglises. Not wishing to importune him, I saved them up until the collection was of decent length, and posted them at the beginning of November 1970. He died, however, a week later.

Although I regret, on personal grounds, not having met de Gaulle my regret is mitigated by the thought that personal acquaintance, and exposure to the force of his personality, might have interfered with my purpose, which was to treat him as a figure in history, as one would write a biography of, say, Cromwell or Richelieu.

My thanks are also due to M. Georges Albertini for kindly sending me much current material of interest, and especially for introducing me to a number of leading Gaullists; and to M. Boris Souvarine, who kindly sent me the typescript of the late General Odic's unpublished memoirs.

The bulk of the British official documents relating to the Second World War was only made available at the Public Records Office, London, about the time this work was being completed. I do not believe they would have affected my interpretation of events.

Finally, I must record my thanks to Mr Frank Shakespeare, formerly head of the United States Information Agency, and Mr Eugene Rosenfeld, of the American Embassy in London, for procuring State Department publications relating to wartime meetings in which General de Gaulle was involved.

Brian Crozier

1973

Part I ⚜ The Enigma of De Gaulle

Chapter 1 ✤ The Man

The presence was crushing. The ruin of a military face, laden with years, wisdom, cunning and rancour, was perched almost incongruously on a massive pear-shaped body. The eyes, which but for vanity would have been hidden behind thick lenses, peered disconcertingly at the visitor. The voice, though old, was a noble compound of the Paris *faubourgs*, the barrack square and the lecture room. Everything about him was beyond the normal measure – his height, his intellect, his memory. When he fixed you, in the flesh or on the little screen – even through the printed word – there was no god in sight but Charles de Gaulle.

This hyperbolic personage twice flashed across French history, casting a gigantic shadow in which lesser figures were at times only faintly visible. Although always known as *mon Général*, even in the highest civilian office of the French Republic, his military career was honourable rather than distinguished, the fortunes of war having denied him the opportunities of ultimate fame. He spent much of the Great War in a German prison camp, having been left for dead on the battlefield after a desperate wound. The Second World War brought him rapid battle promotion, but only to a temporary rank in the lowest grade of general officer, and after the fall of France, he fought the remainder of the war as a politician and statesman, not as a soldier. In earlier military life, much of it on boring garrison duties, he had achieved distinction as an intellectual: a writer and an historian. A prophet also, as events were to show.

This was a man of heroic stature and the adulation or hatred he provoked was of appropriate scale. In a permanent sense, de Gaulle was a hero to millions of ordinary Frenchmen (and, even more, to French women) who had tired of the antics of politicians and who longed for a leader who would tell foreigners where they might no longer trespass. He was also a hero to the "unconditional" Gaullists – that is, to those who, for opportunistic or idealistic motives, would say that the general was right whatever he said or did. At various times, he was also a hero to followers who later turned against him because he disappointed their particular hopes.

To these, and to those who were against him anyway, he was a monster. Among the former were many supporters of *Algérie Française*; among the latter, many supporters of Vichy and much of the French *Patronat*. For the extremes of contradictory passion which his name aroused, and in certain other obvious respects, his career invites comparison with that of General Franco. But there was a deep and significant difference between Franco Spain and Gaullist France. Franco came to power as the outcome of a bloody civil war, after which his opponents were either exiled or liquidated. France avoided a civil war, but only just; for paying off old scores between resisters and collaborators after the Second World War approximated to one. Indeed there were liquidations in France and some famous trials – of which those of Pétain and Laval were the most notorious – but the shedding of compatriots' blood was on a far smaller scale than in Spain. Apart from some collaborators and some "French Algeria" politicians and army officers, most of de Gaulle's antagonists remained in France. For that reason, opposition to him was always stronger at home than opposition to Franco in Spain.

His appeal, however, was always immense, and in 1945 and 1958 overwhelming. He had to an extraordinary degree the capacity to transcend individual groups by stirring up patriotic sentiments among people to whom patriotism meant different things. Many Vichyists rallied round him (and showed it by supporting his rally of the French people), partly through love of the paternalistic authority which Pétain had represented for them, and which they now sought in the younger man. Although the monarchists shunned him, he strongly appealed to residual royalist sentiment among Republicans, since he was so clearly an uncrowned monarch. At the same time, he could be seen as the "defender" and "saviour" of the Republic. Although a section of the army rebelled against him, the bulk of it remained faithful: another source of appeal was to those who were nostalgic for another Bonaparte. Among the many paradoxes of de Gaulle is that he symbolised, for some, authority and legitimacy, for others, glory and adventure.

Another paradox was this. On the one hand, de Gaulle, who came of a line of minor aristocrats and *bourgeois*, and was a practising Catholic, appealed to the *bien-pensants* of conservative France; on the other hand, his family was poor and he despised the *bourgeoisie* and the bosses of the *Patronat*, so that he was able to compete with the Communist party for the voters of the left. In this respect, too, he was a "bridge", for the French are both conservative and revolutionary: their conservatism delays necessary reforms, so that revolution becomes inevitable.

4

The popular image of him abroad, to which his enemies at home contributed, was that of a dictator. But this was misleading. His claim to be the defender of the legitimacy of the Republic inhibited him from asserting, in the full and formal sense, a dictatorship. Other inhibiting factors were the French tradition of liberty and the relative weakness of the authoritarian tradition in comparison with, say, Spain or Germany. He was an autocrat by disposition and character, who exercised his authority through a compelling personality and a uniquely subtle political skill. He was, too, an illusionist or magician, adept at creating a sense of achievement when nothing, in fact, had been done. And with all that, he was of course a consummate actor, and an orator of unusual power and nobility of style.

As long ago as 1932, de Gaulle set out his master-ideas on the requirements of leadership in the most important of his shorter works, *Le Fil de l'Epée* – "The Edge of the Sword". (It is a linguistic irony, by the way, that the French language, de Gaulle's vehicle for this richly subtle and allusive study of the qualities of a leader, lacks a word for "leadership".) Literally translated, these requirements sound strangely alien, though intelligible, in English: the magnetism of confidence, and even of illusion; the elevation of the leader's aims and his contempt for contingencies, leaving to the mass the care of details; the isolation of grandeur[1] and renunciation of happiness. The young de Gaulle knew of course, or felt in his bones, that a time would come when he would act out the part he then wrote. Men of destiny, as we know to our cost, have this habit of writing well in advance the history they plan to make. When Charles de Gaulle was young, his intelligence did not go unnoticed, but his fixed ideas of grandeur were generally ascribed to an overweening vanity. Undeflected from a chosen course, he carried his ideas with him through two wars, the London period, the Algiers period, the Fighting French triumph, the sudden resignation, the years in the wilderness of Colombey-les-Deux-Eglises and the return to power (though he disguised the fact) on the back of a higher-ranking general – Salan – who looked to him to do things he had no intention of doing.

When the second call came in 1958, those who facilitated his return to power were soon to learn the meaning of some of the more devastating notions of *Le Fil de l'Epée*, such as his contemptuous dismissal of "the walkers-on of the hierarchy, parasites who absorb everything and give nothing in return ... safeguarding their careers as civil servants, their promotion as soldiers or their ministers' portfolios". To de Gaulle, in

[1] The French word *grandeur* comprehends the English "greatness" and "grandeur"; the English word "grandeur" is mostly used in this double sense throughout this work.

5

1958 as in 1932, there was no prestige for such as these, but only "the deference that comes with custom". When de Gaulle reigned in the Elysée Palace those dismissive words were still true, in his eyes, of his ministers and even of his soldiers. But it was hardly true or just to call his higher civil servants parasites, for it was they – the hard-worked men in the shadows – who really governed France from the confines of de Gaulle's Elyseum.

For all its frivolous associations, there was a certain aptness in this choice of a dwelling place for an uncrowned monarch. Beyond the little gates and the watchful *gardes Républicains* lies a gravel quadrangle, and beyond that, not the world of Watteau and Fragonard appropriate to the rococo interior (except for visiting dignitaries), but the austere cerebral world of the technocrats – the *Polytechniciens* and *Normaliens*, the *hauts fonctionnaires* who gave Gaullism its underlying structure. For the Elysée has in its day been the home not only of an emperor, a courtesan – Madame de Pompadour – and foreign kings, but of that technocrat of the pretechnocratic age, the financier Beaujon, who lived there in 1773.

It was said, and not untruly, that de Gaulle's technocrats constituted a parallel government. The essence of the Fifth Republic, tailored to the measurements of this exceptional man, lay in the fact that the Prime Minister was not the president of the Council of Ministers. The president of de Gaulle's Republic also presided over the Council of Ministers – and in a dominant way not matched by the weaker presidents of earlier republics when chairing such occasions. Nor was the large and un-wieldy *Conseil des Ministres* in the British sense, a cabinet. When the ministers met in council, they were there *en masse*, not at the Hôtel Matignon, where the Prime Minister worked, but at the Elysée.

The agenda would have been decided in advance – by General de Gaulle. The decisions would have been taken in advance – by General de Gaulle. And the real purpose of the gathering of the council was not to thrash out a policy that had already been determined, but to discuss and report on problems and policies, then take note of policy decisions, the better to execute them. In effect, the visible government executed the orders of the invisible one.

This was what happened, yet in a sense it is an exaggeration to say that there was a parallel government. For visible or invisible, the men who helped de Gaulle reach decisions or carry out his orders owed their positions entirely to the president of the Fifth Republic. In that sense, all were equal in their inequality, and only one was more equal than the others. In that sense, too, there was only one man in de Gaulle's govern-ment: the presiding president.

6

De Gaulle did not of course invent the Elysée system. Some of it he inherited from the long line of under-powered presidents of the Third and Fourth Republics, notably the departments charged with protocol and other ceremonial matters. But the machinery that had been geared to the needs of ornamental presidents was inadequate for those of a man who wanted to rule as well as symbolise. The new Elysée was expanded to meet those wider needs. Under de Gaulle, the Elysée's staff comprised four organs: the *cabinet* (in the French sense of the term, meaning a private secretariat for the president): the secretariat-general; the department for African and Malagasy affairs; and the private general staff.

The *cabinet* regulated the general's personal life, his appointments, the audiences he granted (to which great importance was attached), receptions, dinners and lunches, and journeys. The department for African and Malagasy affairs, in effect, maintained the personal and public links between the general and the African empire he had emancipated, originally known as the Community, and later – when all its African members opted for independence – more realistically as the *ex*-Community. There was nevertheless a strangeness about the presence of this department at the Elysée, and the incumbent in General de Gaulle's time, Jacques Foccart, a much parachuted ex-Resistance man and an old faithful, was also – and primarily – in charge of secret departments covering intelligence and security. Algerian affairs were handled outside the Elysée, by a special office.

The real parallel government was the secretariat-general, whose personnel comprised some fifteen high officials, each of whom had charge of one or more departments corresponding to ministries. The most important dealt with finance, the interior, foreign affairs, education, scientific research and information. Unusual qualities were required of the scarcely known technocrats who manned the secretariat-general. They had to be prepared to work long hours, to produce in written form with unerring accuracy and sometimes at an almost impossible speed the facts, figures, and arguments with which General de Gaulle would later confront the responsible ministers; and of course to bear the brunt of ministerial ire or envy when criticisms or suggestions were resented.

Although de Gaulle valued the *tête-à-tête* over lunch or dinner (a rarely accorded honour) and the small, informal discussion, he wanted everything of importance in writing. To be a Gaullist functionary was thus an exacting occupation for which only a physically fit intellectual *élite* need apply. The most impressive holder of the key office of secretary-general was Etienne Burin des Roziers, an Oxonian ex-ambassador who

7

had belonged to de Gaulle's innermost circle from 1945. It was a punishing job, with an awe-inspiring daily dosage of reading, embracing all the diplomatic telegrams and all the Bills; all the notes, reports and dossiers prepared by the high officials under him. At the Elysée, under the shadow of the president himself, he was the biggest of the "big four" – the others were the head of the *cabinet*, who, besides arranging the general's appointments, had his remaining time full listening to those whom the general declined to receive; the head of the department of African and Malagasy affairs; and the head of the private general staff, once called the *maison militaire*, and later restyled the *état-major particulier*. Everything military, including relations with NATO, nuclear research for military ends, and the transmission of orders to the general's aides-de-camp, came under the head of the private general staff.

These, then, were the organs, but how did they pulsate, gestate, digest, or otherwise function? The secret was known, at least to a few, but shrouded in mystery. It consisted of a procedure evolved for de Gaulle's purposes and known as "restricted councils". Nobody but the participants knew what went on at these meetings which, by definition, were small. The written word, essential to de Gaulle in other respects, was out of its element in this context: there was no agenda for the restricted councils, and no record was kept either of the proceedings or of the identities of participants. The high officials and their departmental chiefs were constantly producing memoranda for de Gaulle. Whenever the general felt a question had ripened sufficiently, he called a restricted council.

Strictly, the system did exist before de Gaulle, in the form of *Conseils interministériels*; but de Gaulle included civil servants and indeed anybody he chose, as well as ministers, in his *conseils restreints*. The originality of the system as revised under General de Gaulle lay in its expansion to duplicate and anticipate the work of the ministries. Regular restricted councils were held on military, African and Malagasy, and Algerian affairs; and less frequent ones on economic and financial affairs, education, scientific research, public works, radio and television, agriculture, and foreign policy.

On paper, the system looked a perfect recipe for secret and absolute rule, and the high officials like overworked men at the beck and call of a tyrant. But de Gaulle was *sui generis* and made short shrift of preconceived notions. Though an exacting taskmaster who made a fetish of punctuality, he did not expect his advisers to be yes-men. By definition, indeed, they were not: he hand picked the best administrative brains, then expected them to argue with him if need be, knowing always that in the end he would make the decisions alone. Nor was it always as

8

militarily efficient as it looked. Too often, the ageing man at the helm merely read a report, endorsed it as "seen" and took no action; and just as often, a decision was taken, but somewhere between the thrusting high official and a more devious minister, the decision trickled out into a dry creek of immobility. "It is as though," a prominent Gaullist told me, "you were on a ship sailing for the North Pole and an officer put a piece of paper before the captain proposing a change of direction to the South Pole. The captain reads it, marks it 'seen', and the ship sails on heading north."

For de Gaulle, who was already fifty when he achieved national and world fame, was an old man when he returned to power; and therein lay his tragedy. A tragedy of hopes deferred and belated opportunities, of obsolete visions and frustrating realities. In his relatively short period of supreme office, de Gaulle consolidated the claim to immortality he had already staked in 1940 as an unknown junior general, but he achieved less than he had hoped or than had been expected of him. Like Bonaparte, de Gaulle came to fame and power as the consequence of a great national upheaval. But Bonaparte was in his twenties when opportunity knocked; de Gaulle was well into middle age. Nor was history kind to de Gaulle in its gift of a century in which to operate.

It was given to de Gaulle to revitalise France; but the France he revitalised was dwarfed by two super-powers in a bi-polar world. Napoleonic France could dominate Europe as Gaullist France could not. Nor was the divided and demoralised people whom de Gaulle to some extent regenerated and united, a match for his dreams of grandeur. All his life, as the general himself put it, he had a "certain idea of France"; but he could never hide his contempt for the French people, who perennially disappointed him by their patent unworthiness of the country of his vision. Nothing written today can diminish the aura of General de Gaulle's wartime exploit. But history may well record the verdict that as a writer, he wrote too little; as a soldier, he fought too little; and as a statesman, he came too late.

When a man has become a living legend, when he has deliberately chosen the solitary path to greatness, when every word and gesture is weighed and calculated in advance for its effect upon others, it becomes difficult indeed to pierce the public armour to reach the flesh and blood beneath. De Gaulle had a few intimates but no friends. Even the earliest Gaullist memoirs are suspect, since they were written by followers who hoped to create a legend and succeeded. As with other great names, many of the anecdotes about him are apocryphal. But all, whether true or false, are consistent. His language in private, generously laced with barrack-square coarseness, was marked by an abrasive and sardonic wit. His sufferance of fools was short-lived. As a schoolboy and a subaltern, he was liked, but usually at a distance: already, his height, the singularity of his mind, and his vocation of solitude set him apart from the others. His character training began early, under the fond but professorial sternness of his father; and he consciously trained himself for greatness. Adversity completed the process, with his wartime captivity in Germany and later, the death of his handicapped daughter Anne. His marriage was felicitous, his private life untouched by scandal.

Perhaps, after all, there was no enigma – except in the minds of lesser men who found it hard to conceive such tenacity of purpose, such apparent perverseness in the pursuit of the unattainable, such constancy in striving to reproduce in real life the plans so carefully described in a literary youth. To such as these, de Gaulle was frequently disconcerting. But he was so only to those who expected him to behave as timidly or inconsistently as lesser men might. To those who knew him best, or studied him most assiduously, there was no enigma: very early in life, Charles de Gaulle knew where he wanted to go, and in later life, he did or attempted to do what he had always said he would do.

Chapter 2 ✤ Historical Prologue

Charles de Gaulle was born in 1890 at the height of the Panama scandal, and in the wake of the Boulanger crisis and the Wilson affair.

The common background to these events was the Bonapartist experiment of Prince Louis-Napoleon, who became Napoleon III and as such a precursor of the twentieth-century dictators. Tiny in stature and pompous in appearance, Napoleon III owed his success in gaining power at least as much to the magic of his name and the nostalgia for recent imperial glory as to his talent as a conspirator and self-propagandist. The people of France undoubtedly wanted him to be, first, their prince-president and later, their emperor. There was no need for him to fake the plebiscite by which they overwhelmingly approved of the *coup d'état* he had carried out in December 1851. For eight years or so, he gave them sound, authoritarian government, economic expansion and even foreign successes – in particular, the defeat of Russia, in alliance with England, in the Crimean War. He also gave them, as had the first Napoleon, a stifling of political liberty. The splendour of his court, however, contributed to his popularity, as it had to that of the first Napoleon. Certainly, the initial stability of the Second Empire contributed to its economic successes. A depression in 1846, aggravated by revolutionary violence in 1848, turned into a surge of expansion. King Louis-Philippe (1830–48) had given France a railway system; Napoleon III trebled it and more, making of Paris more than ever the scintillating capital of France. Credit institutions and joint stock banks, such as the Société Générale, were founded and flourished. Small investors proliferated. By 1870 France was a notable industrial power.

It was in foreign affairs that Napoleon III's judgment was most deficient. His interventions in Italy, Austria and Mexico were ill-judged and costly adventures. The dominant political and military reality of Europe after the seven weeks' war of 1866 was the emergence of Prussia as a great power. Napoleon III allowed himself to be goaded by Bismarck into a disastrous declaration of war on 19 July 1870. The outcome was the invasion of France, the capitulation of the French army and the collapse of the Second Empire. Thus, for the second time in less than a century, a Napoleon had brought both grandeur and humiliation to France.

This second disaster, worse even than 1815 in its consequences for France, might have seemed enough. But it did not deter yet another Bonapartist adventure – that of General Boulanger. General Boulanger was popular on a number of counts, none of them historically impressive. On the positive side, he had fought bravely in Africa, in Italy and in Cochin-China. As minister of War in 1886 under the Third Republic, he cut a dashing figure that endeared him to women, and made speeches that flattered the crowd. There was a negative asset as well: one of his wounds was received as fighting began in Paris in the wake of defeat in the Franco-Prussian war. This circumstance saved him from involvement in repressing the revolutionary Communards. He was thus acceptable to the mob as well as to the military hierarchy.

Boulanger's Bonapartist moment came, however, on the crest of the wave of anti-Prussian patriotic sentiment. Boulanger crystallised the popular mood of *revanchisme*. The instrument of France's revenge against the Germans was to be Boulanger's "republicanised" army. Overnight, Boulanger became "General Revanche", when Bismarck, in a *Reichstag* speech in January 1887, named him as the greatest obstacle

11

to good relations between France and Germany. In May, however, the ministry fell. Instantly, Boulanger turned to conspiracy. The Wilson affair – one of the juicy scandals so characteristic of French republics – gave him his chance. President Grévy's son-in-law, Daniel Wilson, was found to have been conducting a thriving traffic in honours and decorations, which he sold from the Elysée Palace itself, thus economising on office space. High personages were implicated, and the long crisis that followed this discovery forced the resignation of the President and his government.

The Royalists and Bonapartists decided that only Boulanger could save France. In January 1889, Boulanger was elected to parliament with a big majority. The *coup d'état* that was to bring him to power was prepared. Had Boulanger been as resolute as his oratory indicated, it might have succeeded. Instead, his essential frivolity and laziness came uppermost. Losing his nerve, he walked out on his followers. Not long after, threatened with prosecution, Boulanger fled to Brussels. Appropriately, it was All Fools' day. Thirty months later, he committed suicide on the grave of his mistress.

In 1889, at the height of the Boulangist crisis, the Panama Canal Company crashed spectacularly. The panic-stricken shareholders appealed to the government to protect their interests. The director, Ferdinand de Lesseps, of Suez Canal fame, was charged with corruption, along with some of his colleagues. The charges remained unproven, but rumours that deputies had been bribed by Jewish financiers persisted. One of the financiers, Baron de Reinach, was found dead; and another, Cornelius Hertz, fled to England, lending apparent substance to the allegations. The scandal, on top of Boulanger's disastrous failure and the earlier Wilson scandal, drove many Frenchmen to the political extremes. On the right, there was a wave of virulent anti-Semitism, echoed some years later in the notorious Dreyfus affair; on the left, especially in the provinces – ever distrustful of Paris – many voters took the view that the Republic's politicians were incurably corrupt.

The most important fact of European history at the time when de Gaulle entered it, however, was the emergence of Prussia as the dominant land power in Europe. *Revanchisme* was in the air in his boyhood and youth (significantly, the penultimate chapter of his *La France et son Armée* is entitled *"Vers la Revanche"*) and the concept of a permanent see-saw struggle for European hegemony between Germany and France permeates General de Gaulle's early writings. The history of de Gaulle's middle and later years is marked by his stubborn resistance to the changed realities of power politics after 1940: the emergence of Russia and America as the overwhelming powers, the traumatic paradox of a defeated France with a place among the victors (itself one of de Gaulle's greatest achievements), and the consequent moral ascendancy of France over an economically resurgent but truncated Germany; and the enfeeblement of Great Britain.

Part II ⚜ Historian and Thinker
1890–1939

Chapter 1 ✤ Pupil of the Jesuits 1890–1909

Aged ten, Charles de Gaulle had already formed his "certain idea of France"; at thirteen, he had chosen a military calling.

The family background of his childhood was itself, of course, the product of a long heredity of solid northern burghers and petty nobility with a tradition of duty and service to the State. His nearest forbears included a literary grandmother and a scientific uncle. His father, a teacher, presided over an austere but loving household, in which money, it is said, was held in quiet contempt.[1]

But liberalism, in this unostentatious home, went hand in hand with propriety and Catholic observance. It was at first considered normal to defend the accusers of Dreyfus, the Jewish officer condemned for alleged treason; but Charles de Gaulle's father valued justice above class solidarity, and soon started defending the accused.[2]

The de Gaulles came from Flanders, Champagne and Burgundy. A fifteenth-century de Gaulle fought against the king of England; an eighteenth-century descendant was Prosecutor to the parliament of Paris.[3]

In 1835 the de Gaulles of Burgundy renewed their ancestral links with French Flanders, when Julien-Philippe de Gaulle married Joséphine-Anne-Marie Maillot, whose family came from Lille, though it owned tobacco factory at Dunkirk. It was an interesting union. Socially, it united a Burgundian family of nobles and civil servants with a *bourgeois* family of the industrious Flemish north. Personally, it joined a historian and a writer. For it was Julien-Philippe de Gaulle who was the author of the *Nouvelle Histoire de Paris et de ses Environs*. A palaeographer, Julien-Philippe had compiled an elaborate history of the de Gaulle family, which remains unpublished. His wife Joséphine, General de Gaulle's paternal

---

[1] Pierre Galante, *Le Général* (Paris, 1968), p. 47 (henceforth, Galante).
[2] J. R. Tournoux, *Pétain and de Gaulle* (Paris, 1964), p. 39n. (henceforth, Tournoux, Pétain).
[3] For a fuller account of de Gaulle's genealogy, *see* Georges Cattaui, *Charles de Gaulle* (l'Homme et son Destin) (Paris, 1960), pp. 11–17, (henceforth, Cattaui).

grandmother, was, however, a more distinguished literary figure. Intellectually emancipated at a time when women of good family were not encouraged to do anything more ambitious than dabble in the arts, she became the editor of a review entitled *Correspondance des Familles* in which she was bold enough to publish essays by the revolutionary socialist Jules Vallès. She herself wrote eulogies of a more serious socialist, the philosopher Proudhon. Yet Joséphine Maillot was far from being a socialist. A fervent Catholic, she wrote more than a dozen works of piety, whose high moral tone was much praised at the time. Her versatility was indeed remarkable, for she made her name with a novel that still finds interested readers: *Adhémar de Belcastel*. Moreover, her works include a life of Chateaubriand and another of *O'Connell, Libérateur de l'Irlande*. Both biographies have a curious bearing on the taste and achievements of her grandson, for Charles de Gaulle became a great admirer of Chateaubriand, while the thesis of her book on O'Connell provides a parallel with de Gaulle's life. In it, she praised the Irish patriot for having made a revolution without bloodshed, and a settlement that respected law and order.

Three sons were born of the marriage, and each in his way was remarkable. The eldest, Charles, was a chronic invalid who found relief in a life-long study of the Celts. He learned Welsh and Breton, published poems in the latter under the name of *Barz Bro-C'hall* – Breton for "the Bard de Gaulle", and wrote a work on the Celts of the nineteenth century. A visionary as well as a scholar, he dreamed of forming a union of the Celts of all the world, associating the Bretons with the Welsh, the Irish and the Scots.

His brother Jules was to become France's foremost entomologist, and catalogued 5,000 varieties of French bees and wasps. The third brother, Henri, born in 1848, married a cousin, Jeanne Maillot-Delannoy, in her native town of Lille on 2 August 1886. A pious young woman, two of whose sisters were nuns, Jeanne had a recent Irish and Scottish ancestry. A tall, distinguished-looking man with a slight stoop, Henri de Gaulle had chosen a military career and had passed the entrance examination to the Polytechnique, but changed his plans when his father died suddenly, leaving him in charge of the family. He was twenty-two, and it was 1870. France faced defeat, and Henri de Gaulle answered Gambetta's call for volunteers. Since the Germans did not recognise them, they were publicly called "sharpshooters". Young Henri was wounded, and a medal – later treasured by his son – marked the occasion.

When peace returned in 1870, Henri de Gaulle would have liked to resume his studies. But necessity made him earn his living as a teacher.

He was thirty-eight before he felt sufficiently established to take on the responsibility of marriage. Madame de Gaulle chose to have her babies, as she had chosen to get married, at Lille. The first was a son, Xavier, named after the Jesuit saint of the parish. Henri's brother Charles – the Celtic visionary – died shortly after, at barely thirty. And the second son was named after him. Charles de Gaulle was born on 22 November 1890, in the house of his maternal grandparents, 9 Rue Princesse. Next day, he was baptised in the austere Carmelite church of St André, with the Christian names Charles André Joseph Marie. Though Charles de Gaulle was thus by birth a Lillois, he was given a Parisian upbringing.

When Charles was born, his father was teaching philosophy, mathematics and literature in the College of the Immaculate Conception, founded by the Jesuit fathers at 389 Rue de Vaugirard. And a year later, he was appointed director (*préfet*) of studies. It was a bad time to be teaching for the Jesuits. In the wake of the Dreyfus scandal, a wave of anti-militarism and anti-clericalism swept the Third Republic, whose leaders linked the army and the Church as symbols of reaction. The Premier, Emile Combes, a prominent freemason, was determined to end the privileges of the religious orders and transform the Concordat with the Vatican into a "Discordat". On 9 December 1905, on the eve of his fall from office, a law he had sponsored severed all ties between Church and State. From that day, the Republic would no longer pay priests and bishops; nor was the Church allowed to own property, which the State seized as its own. Lay committees were set up to administer church affairs in every parish. The Combes law was denounced in the papal encyclical *Vehementor Nos*, and in the more pious regions of France – in Brittany, in Auvergne and in Flanders – defiant Catholics barricaded themselves in the churches to prevent inventories by the hated fiscal agents of the State. In several places, troops had to be used to evict them.

The Jesuit fathers had to abandon the College of the Immaculate Conception, and took refuge in Belgium. One day, the police commissioner of the Vaugirard district, with the authority of the tricolour sash of office, called at the college and asked to see "Father" de Gaulle, who, as director of studies, was in charge of the diminished establishment. M. de Gaulle received him in his normal garb – frock-coat and pale yellow gloves. "I am not 'Father de Gaulle'," he said with his usual dignity. "You have no business here."

"Not at all," said the policeman, vaguely disconcerted, "you are a Jesuit in civilian clothes."

M. de Gaulle was not a man to lose his temper or equanimity. With patient courtesy, he enquired: "Would you like me to introduce you to my wife and five children?"[4]

There was a cruel irony in Henri de Gaulle's minor confrontation with the police. The Radicals were out to punish the military and Catholic establishment, which they blamed for the mad adventures of Napoleon III, the defeat of France by the Prussians and the Dreyfus affair. But Henri de Gaulle was a nationalist and a practising Christian through passionate moral conviction, and not because those were the views of the class into which he was born. Above all, he was a man of justice who became convinced of the innocence of Dreyfus. The *affaire* had split France. For two years, from 1894, a French staff officer and playboy, Major Esterhazy, had been selling information to the Germans. French counter-intelligence accused the young Jewish officer Captain Alfred Dreyfus of the crime, but would probably have dropped the charge for lack of evidence if a vicious anti-Semite, Edouard Drumont, author of the explosive best-seller *La France juive*, had not got wind of the affair and published a charge that wealthy Jews were trying to protect a traitor. Forged documents sent Dreyfus to Devil's Island for life (though he was later vindicated). One of his staunchest defenders was the nationalist poet Charles Péguy – one of the major influences in Charles de Gaulle's life. The Dreyfus affair was a table topic in the de Gaulle household, and years later Charles de Gaulle was to write this passage about it in his book on the French army:

> By a kind of fatality, at the very moment when the spirit of the public is tending to take its distance from the army, there bursts the crisis that is most likely to magnify evil intentions. In this lamentable trial, nothing that could poison the passions was to be lacking. The probability of a judicial error, supported by forgeries, irresponsibilities, abuses on the part of the prosecution, but rejected with horror by those who, by faith or for reasons of State, are determined to maintain the infallibility of a hierarchy devoted to the service of the fatherland; an exasperating obscurity, in which a thousand muddled incidents, intrigues, confessions, retractions, duels, suicides, subsidiary trials, enrage and constantly throw off the scent the two rival packs; an unhealthy frenzy, where that elementary respect for the symbol of their power in which the divided French manage to unite, sinks helter-skelter along with mutual respect, convictions, friendships.[5]

Charles de Gaulle was too young by a few years to understand what

[4] Galante, p. 41.
[5] *La France et son Armée* (Paris, 1938, 1965), pp. 243–4 (henceforth, De Gaulle, *France*).

was going on at the time, but old enough to realise later what the Dreyfus affair meant to his father's generation. Shame and defeat; patriotism and the nation; faith and religion – these were the themes of Professor de Gaulle's paternal guidance. The affair had tarnished the army's prestige: many officers resigned their commissions, and applications for entrance into the Saint-Cyr Military Academy fell by half.[6]

The Radicals, who in Gambetta's day had been fiercely patriotic, turned anti-militaristic. The Waldeck–Rousseau government (1899–1902) – though relatively mild in comparison with the successor government of Emile Combes – brought in legislation depriving the officer corps of the power to make its own promotions, and anti-clerical laws that forced thousands of monks and nuns into exile.

It was against this background that Charles de Gaulle heard his father's story of the wound he had sustained when the Germans were besieging Paris, and his mother's talk of her parents in tears at the news that the vainglorious Marshal Bazaine had capitulated with all his forces. That stern moralist, Henri de Gaulle, never failed to point the contrast between the ideal of a grave and faithful Christian France, and the unworthiness of the citizens who fell short of it – a theme that was to dominate General de Gaulle's nationalist thinking. Shame and honour, indeed, alternated in France at large and at the de Gaulle table. There was Sedan, and Dreyfus; there was also, in a relatively minor vein, Fashoda, where a bold but unfortunate young French officer, Captain Marchand, had been forced to turn tail when leading an expedition to challenge Britain's hold on the Upper Nile in 1899.[7] But against these symbols of national shame were names that spelt France's honour. One, much talked about at home, was that of General Faidherbe, a Lillois like de Gaulle's mother, and the conqueror of Senegal. Others held to have brought honour to the French name were thinkers and writers: the philosopher Henri Bergson, and his teacher Boutroux; the Dreyfusard journalist Bernard Lazare; the Dreyfusard poet Péguy; Péguy's friend, the officer and writer Ernest Psichari; the poet and playwright Edmond Rostand; and that wild and unpredictable romantic, the ex-Boulangiste, Maurice Barrès, whose shattering novel, *Du sang, de la volupté, et de la mort* ('Blood, Sensuality and Death'), was published when Charles de Gaulle was four, and who lived on to campaign passionately for the restoration of Alsace and Lorraine and to write a chronicle of the First World War.

[6] Gordon Wright, *France in Modern Times* (London, 1962) (henceforth, Wright).
[7] De Gaulle, père, thought "perfidious" too mild a word for Queen Victoria's Albion (Tournoux, *Pétain*, p. 39).

As a boy, Charles de Gaulle's favourite poet was Rostand. On his tenth birthday, his father took him to see Rostand's *l'Aiglon*, a patriotic play which so fascinated the boy that on coming home he announced he would become a soldier.[8] Later, he learned the same writer's *Cyrano de Bergerac* by heart. Péguy was a literary and patriotic love of later adolescence, and lasted all de Gaulle's life. This austere and mystical figure, deeply influenced by Bergson, from whom he derived a distaste for ready-made thinking, wrote intricately skilful verse, much of it on the Joan of Arc theme, in which he expressed his vision of France as the symbol of Christian virtues. His view of a mother France, the duty of whose sons was to serve her, was a lasting influence on de Gaulle.

Charles had three brothers and a sister. Xavier was the eldest, Charles the second; his sister was named Marie-Agnès; the youngest boy was Pierre, and Jacques came between Charles and Pierre. To accommodate this large family, Henri de Gaulle had bought an austere but impressive property called La Ligerie, in the Dordogne valley, and there they spent their summer holidays. The children were given the option of one book each to take away, and Charles, on the first journey south, chose a history of France.[9]

Though affectionate toward his parents, Charles had an aggressive temper, and his father often chastised him physically.[10] He appears to have taken the warlike games natural to boys of their ages more seriously than the others. One day Pierre, the youngest, came in tears to his mother, who asked him what was the matter. The boy replied, "Charles has beaten me." Asked why, he explained, "We were at war. I was the secret agent. I was captured. I had a message. Instead of carrying out the orders of the commanding general . . ."

"What general?"

"Charles! Instead of swallowing the message, I gave it to the enemy."[11]

On another occasion, Charles refused to surrender the crown of France to Xavier who had tired of always being the emperor of Germany, exclaiming indignantly, "Never! France belongs to me."

Apocryphal or not, these stories are in character. Galante, who records the second anecdote, goes on to say that when de Gaulle was in the second form (equivalent to the British upper fifth) he came home one day to announce that he was indeed determined to be a soldier: "I have taken my decision. I shall prepare for Saint-Cyr, I shall become a soldier." Until then, de Gaulle appears to have given unexpectedly little attention

[8] Cattaui, p. 20.   [9] Galante, p. 47.   [10] Tournoux, *Pétain*, p. 25.
[11] Galante's version of a story also recounted by other biographers. A different version appears in Cattaui, p. 31.

to his formal studies. Absorbed by his martial games, by adventure stories, and by his beloved poets and writers, he spent more time writing verses of his own than studying. His mother thought piano lessons would encourage a more studious discipline, but was soon disappointed by his lack of interest (although he loved to listen to music). His astonishing memory – which he had already begun to train by speaking words spelt backwards – usually carried him through. But his father was obliged to warn him that if he did not settle down to serious work, he could not hope to pass the entrance examination to Saint-Cyr.

Charles was fourteen. He listened to the warning, set to work and came top of his class. But at fifteen he allowed himself a last poetic fling. Working in secret, he wrote a sketch in verse, *An Ill-fated Meeting*, recording the misfortunes of a naïve passer-by, deprived of his possessions by a clever rogue.[12] He sent the playlet to a literary review, which offered him a choice between a fee of twenty-five francs and publication of his work. Characteristically, he chose publication.

He was growing fast and already towered above his classmates. Though quarrelsome and a natural leader, he was not without a sense of humour. Taking advantage of the fact he was already as tall as an adult, he chose a suitable disguise, and knocked at the door of his own home one day, announcing himself as "General Faidherbe". The choice of identification with this conquering general was perhaps significant.

In 1907, he was sent to the Belgian side of the frontier to finish his secondary studies in the Antoine College, which the exiled French Jesuits had set up there. But he returned to Paris after a year to attend Stanislas College, where he prepared for the entrance examination to Saint-Cyr. And in August 1909, he learned that he had been accepted. His military life was about to begin.

[12] The text is reproduced in full in Tournoux, *Pétain*, pp. 29 *et seq.*

Chapter 2 ⚜ The Young Officer 1909–1918

Charles de Gaulle became a soldier at a time of industrial unrest, rising nationalism and a philosophical cult of the irrational. Those were his years of maximum awareness. The cloud beyond the horizon was war

– a war yet unnamed, which de Gaulle was not alone in sensing and which many of his elders anticipated with patriotic expectancy.

With marked reluctance, French society was moving into the modern age. An increasingly literate peasantry was beginning to take an interest in the political process, and becoming aware of the power of the peasant vote. Much of French industry retained its artisan character; and the urban workers clung to the right to remain ununionised. One-fifth of them – about a million – had, however, joined the Confédération Générale du Travail (CGT), and thereby opted for syndicalism – that is, for revolutionary militancy. In 1909, the year de Gaulle entered Saint-Cyr, there were more than one thousand strikes throughout the country.[1] France had not yet ceased to be a traditional society, but parts of her were already touched by the twentieth century.

More directly inspired by Marx than by the French Socialist philosophers, the organised workers were in the vanguard of the anti-militarists. In 1906 the CGT adopted a marching order that was to become famous: "Anti-militarist and anti-patriotic propaganda must become ever more intense and even bolder." Commenting later on this period in *La France et son Armée* Charles de Gaulle noted disdainfully that "the active wing of the Social Movement", scorning Fourier, Proudhon and other French philosophers, had enrolled itself under the banner of Karl Marx. In the next paragraph, he notes sorrowfully that the working masses were repudiating the warlike sentiment previously associated with the Revolution. "A considerable fraction of the people joins the International. No enemies, other than the enemies of the proletariat!"[2]

Nor were the organised workers alone in the wave of anti-militarism that swept France in the first years of the century. A schoolmaster named Gustave Hervé launched a vitriolic campaign against the army in the trade union press. Denigrating patriotism, pouring scorn on the officers, he called on army recruits to tear down the flag and plant it on a dung heap. On the military issue, as on so many others, however, the French were deeply divided; nor was Marx the only important German influence upon French thought. In the wake of the disasters of 1870, the national mood of introspection turned to the study of German political organisation and German culture in a search for causes and possible remedies. As de Gaulle put it, Kant, Fichte, Hegel and Nietzsche were being taught in the Sorbonne through third parties. One of the foremost French thinkers of the dying quarter of the nineteenth century, Ernest Renan, cam-

[1] P.-M. de la Gorce, *De Gaulle entre Deux Mondes* (Paris, 1964), p. 35 (henceforth, Gorce).
[2] De Gaulle, *France*, pp. 242–3.